Now You Know:
Where Plants Live

Encyclopaedia Britannica Educational Corporation   Chicago/Toronto

Copyright © 1973
Encyclopaedia Britannica Educational Corporation

All rights reserved   Printed in the United States of America

This work may not be transmitted by television or other devices
or processes nor copied, recast, transformed, or adapted in any manner,
in whole or in part, without a license.
For information regarding a license, write
Encyclopaedia Britannica Educational Corporation, Chicago, Illinois 60611.

Library of Congress Catalog Card Number: 73-75046

International Standard Book Number: 0-87827-103-1

Where Plants Live

Author
Anne Neigoff

Designer
Paul McNear

Artist
James G. Teason

Consultants
Johnnie L. Gentry, Jr., Assistant Curator, Vascular Plants
Field Museum of Natural History
Chicago, Illinois

Deborah Partridge Wolfe, Professor of Education
Queens College, City University of New York
Flushing, New York

Encyclopaedia Britannica Educational Corporation

Almost everywhere in the world,
   in quiet lakes and rushing rivers,
   in deep oceans and on high mountains,
   in hot lands and cold lands,
   plants live and grow.

In the ocean waters, plants are floating.
They are different colors and sizes.
Many plants are so tiny
    that you cannot see just one plant
    without a microscope.

But when many tiny green plants float together,
    they make the water look green.
Small fish and huge whales eat the tiny plants.
The sun shines on the salty ocean
    and helps the plants to grow.

If you stand on a rocky shore
   and look down, down,
   into the ocean waters,
    sometimes you can see a forest growing.
Kelp plants are growing there,
   and many are as tall as trees.
Their thick stems hold fast to the rocks.
Their long blades float in the water,
   and little fish dart in and out
    of their home in the kelp forest.

Look at this quiet pond.

Where are plants growing?
Tall cattails grow up, up, up
   above the water
   and bend in the breeze.

On the water,
   the leaves and flowers
   of water lilies float.

Tiny duckweeds
   float on the water, too.
Down, down in the water,
   pondweeds
   and waterweeds
   live and grow.

Sunlight
  shines through
  the clear water of the pond
  and helps the plants to grow.
The long leaves
  of the waterweeds wave
  as the water
  lifts them gently.

The roots of some water plants
  get food from the soil
  at the bottom of the pond.
Insects and small fish
  live among the stems
  and eat the plants in the water.

9

This desert is hot and dry.
Sometimes rain falls, but the desert sands
 dry quickly under the burning sun.
Plants need water to live.
Can plants live here?

In the desert,
   the seeds of some plants
   rest a long time.
At last the rain pours down,
   splashing and splashing.
Many seeds begin to grow.
New plants are growing
   on the desert.
Flowers are growing
   on other plants.
Soon the desert
   is covered with flowers
   of many colors.
Then the flowers are gone,
   but from their seeds,
   new plants will grow.

Cactus plants grow in the hot desert all year round.
The prickly-pear cactus has roots that spread wide.
When just a little rain falls, the roots soak it up fast.
The prickly-pear cactus has enough water to grow.

The barrel cactus fills with water when the rain falls.
Little by little, it uses up the water until the rain comes again.
Can you tell which barrel cactus is filled with water?

Cactus plants are big and small.
The tall saguaro is the king
  of the cactus plants.

The plants have different shapes and flowers.
But they all can live with just a little water.
They all can live and grow in the desert.

The places where grasses grow
  as far as you can see
  are called the grasslands.
Rain falls on the grasslands,
  but there is not enough rain
  to sink deep into the ground.

Few trees can grow there.
  They need more water.
This grassland is called a prairie.
The green grass rolls on and on,
  and, here and there, flowers grow.

Sometimes the wide prairie looks empty.
But if you look close, you will see
　　the nest of a meadowlark, hidden in the grass.
Then a hawk swoops low,
　　and a gopher runs to its burrow home.

Do you see the little hills on the prairie?
They are the front doors to a prairie-dog town.
The prairie dogs pop their heads out of the front doors
　　to their burrows
　　and go out to eat the prairie grass.

The grass grows tall
  on this windy grassland.
Here and there,
  a few low trees grow.
In the grass you can see paths
  where many animals roam.
They eat the grass
  and make their homes here.

This woodland changes in spring and summer,
autumn and winter.
In the spring, green leaves begin to grow
on the trees.
On the woodland floor, wild flowers grow
as the sun shines down.
Baby animals are born, and birds fly back
from their winter homes in the south.

By summer, the trees are covered with leaves
   that make a thick, green roof over the woodland.
Little sunlight shines through the roof of leaves.
The early spring flowers are gone.
But on the dim, shadowed woodland floor,
   other flowers are opening,
   and mosses, ferns, and mushrooms grow.
Birds sing in the trees and deer nibble the leaves.
Many animals find homes in the summer woodland.

In autumn, the days grow shorter
 and the nights are cool.
The leaves on the woodland trees
 change color.
They blaze red and gold and orange.
Squirrels and deer and chipmunks
 eat the acorns on the oak trees.
Many of the birds fly away.
The colors in the leaves fade
 and the leaves fall from the trees.

In winter, cold winds blow
 through the woodland.
The branches of the trees are bare.
Snow falls and covers the dead leaves
 on the woodland floor.
It is hard for animals to find food
 in the woodland now.
Squirrels hunt for the nuts
 they buried in autumn.
Deer eat bark, nuts, and roots.

It is never winter in the jungle.
The jungle is always hot and wet.
Everywhere you look, there are trees—
    small trees, tall trees, trees of every size.
Leafy vines grow on the trees.
When you look up in the jungle,
    green leaves seem to hide the sun.
But when the sun is high in the blue sky,
    sunlight falls here and there
    on the shady jungle floor.
Ferns, mosses, and lichens grow on the ground
    and on fallen logs and tree trunks.

Many animals find food and homes in the jungle.
Parrots with bright colors live in the treetops.
Tree snakes slide among the leaves,
    and butterflies swoop through the air.
Monkeys chatter in the trees, too.
This jungle is a busy and noisy place.

Some jungle plants climb up and up
   to reach the sunlight.
Woody vines grow quickly.
Often they climb up the trees
   and hang like great ropes
   from one tree to another tree.
The stems of the hanging vines are so strong
   that a man can climb them.

Many plants in the jungle grow on trees.
This orchid grows on a tree branch.
Some of its roots hold on to the branch.
Other special roots take food from the air.
If you stand on the jungle floor,
 you cannot always see the flowers growing
 high on the trees.

On the high peaks of this mountain,
    there is always snow.
It is too cold and windy for trees to grow here,
    but grasses cling to the ground.
Farther down the mountain, the air is not so cold.
The wind blows and blows, but tiny crooked
    spruce and pine trees grow among the rocks.

High on the mountain is a meadow.
When the snow melts and the sun is hot,
    after a few days,
    the ground is covered with flowers.
How small and low the flowers grow!
Only a strong wind can snap their stems.
The plants that grow on a mountain
    are different in many ways,
    but they all can live with the blowing wind.

A cold wind
   blows over the polar lands
   at the top of the world.
Huge blocks of ice
   float in the polar ocean,
   but many tiny plants grow under the ice
   in these waters.
Tiny shrimps
   live in the cold waters
   and eat the plants.

No trees grow near the polar lands,
   but moss and lichens grow.
When summer comes,
   flowers spring up
   from the snow.

Soon summer is over,
 and the flowers are gone.
Reindeer brush away the snow
 with their hoofs
 and eat the moss and lichens.

Wild plants grow in deserts and on mountains,
   in woodlands and jungles,
   in lakes and oceans.
Animals eat the plants.
People plant corn and wheat,
            red tomatoes and green beans,
      and trees on which cherries grow.
How good they taste!

Shady trees and flowers grow in towns
   and cities, too.
They grow in parks and gardens and vacant lots
   and along the streets.
Plants grow in window boxes and pots
   in tall apartment buildings
   and offices and schools.
We like to see green things growing.
What plants are you growing?

Where do these plants live?